Odell Beckham Jr.

By Jon M. Fishman

AMAZING ATHLETES

Lerner Publications ◆ Minneapolis

Lerner Publications Company
A division of Lerner Publishing Group, Inc.
241 First Avenue North
Minneapolis, MN 55401 USA

For reading levels and more information, look up this title at www.lernerbooks.com.

Library of Congress Cataloging-in-Publication Data

Names: Fishman, Jon M., author.
Title: Odell Beckham Jr. / by Jon M. Fishman.
Description: Minneapolis : Lerner Publications, [2017] | Series: Amazing Athletes | Includes
    bibliographical references, webography and index.
Identifiers: LCCN 2016010150 (print) | LCCN 2016011125 (ebook) | ISBN 9781512413359 (lb : alk. paper)
    | ISBN 9781512413656 (pb : alk. paper) | ISBN 9781512413663 (eb pdf)
Subjects: LCSH: Beckham, Odell, Jr., 1992-—Juvenile literature. | Football players—United States—
    Biography—Juvenile literature.
Classification: LCC GV939.B424 F57 2017 (print) | LCC GV939.B424 (ebook) | DDC 796.332092—dc23

LC record available at http://lccn.loc.gov/2016010150

Manufactured in the United States of America
1-39793-21330-3/22/2016

TABLE OF CONTENTS

Odell Beckham Jr. (*right*) reaches for the ball during a 2015 game against the Miami Dolphins.

GIANT HERO

New York Giants **wide receiver** Odell Beckham Jr. stood ready with his knees bent. *Hut, hut!* The **quarterback** called for the play to begin. Odell pushed forward. He dashed into the **end zone** and looked for the ball. He reached up and snatched it out of the air for a touchdown!

Odell and the Giants were playing against the Miami Dolphins on December 14, 2015. Odell's touchdown tied the score, 24–24. The Giants were fighting for a place in the National Football League (NFL) **playoffs**. If they could beat the Dolphins, New York would be tied for first place in their **division**.

Odell (*right*) runs for a touchdown in the second half of the game.

Near the beginning of the fourth quarter, New York got the ball again. Quarterback Eli Manning threw a 12-yard pass.

On the next play, Manning hopped back a few steps. Then he stepped forward and sent the ball flying. It sailed in an arc over the center of the field and dropped into Odell's hands.

The speedy wide receiver was wide open.

Quarterback Eli Manning gets ready to throw the ball.

Odell sprinted toward the end zone. Two Miami players tried to run him down, but they couldn't catch up. It was an 84-yard touchdown for Odell and New York!

Odell danced in the end zone as his teammates gathered to celebrate. Dolphins fans at the stadium in Miami were stunned.

Odell (*left*) celebrates with his teammates after scoring a touchdown.

Their team got the ball two more times, but they couldn't score. The Giants won the game, 31–24. Miami's loss meant they had no chance to make the playoffs.

Odell's big game wasn't a surprise to his fans and people who know him. Miami wide receiver Jarvis Landry played football with Odell in college. Reporters asked Landry about Odell after the game. "Obviously, his performance is something we all expect," Landry said. "He's just continuing to do what he does."

The Mississippi River passes through New Orleans, Louisiana.

TINY TIGER

Odell Cornelious Beckham Jr. was born on November 5, 1992, in New Orleans, Louisiana. His mother, Heather Van Norman, and his father, Odell Beckham Sr., were students at Louisiana State University (LSU). "I was a school baby," Odell said. "They took me to class."

Odell called himself a school baby, but he was also a sports baby. His mother was a track-and-field champion for the LSU Tigers. She helped the school win the outdoor track-and-field national championship in 1991, 1992, and 1993. From 1989 to 1992, Odell's father played **running back** for the LSU football team.

Odell's parents raised him while they studied and trained for their sports. The young boy got to hang around world-class athletes such as Shaquille O'Neal. Shaq played basketball for the school from 1989 to 1992. He and Odell

After college, Shaquille O'Neal won the National Basketball Association (NBA) championship four times. He did it three times with the Los Angeles Lakers and once with the Miami Heat.

Shaquille O'Neal (*center*) played basketball at LSU.

became good friends. Odell said Shaq was like his uncle.

It was no surprise that Odell wanted to be an athlete too. When he was four years old, he ran around his house playing football. He told his mother he was practicing to play **professional** football. "I'm going to be in the NFL," Odell said. He was so sure of himself that his mother believed him.

By 2007, Odell was ready for high school and his first major step toward the NFL. He attended Isidore Newman School in New Orleans. It was a good place for someone who dreamed of playing professional football. NFL superstars Peyton and Eli Manning and their brother, Cooper, had gone there.

NFL quarterbacks Eli Manning (*second from left*) and Peyton Manning (*right*) attended Isidore Newman School.

Odell could do it all on a football field. In addition to wide receiver, he often played quarterback or running back with the **offense**. He also played with the **defense**. Sometimes he even kicked **punts** and **field goals**. But as he grew, Odell realized he had a special talent for catching passes. He decided to focus on playing wide receiver.

In 2010 ESPN ranked Isidore Newman School at the top of a list of high schools that produce the best NFL players.

Football scouts measure how fast players run, among many other things.

HOME AGAIN

In 2009, Odell was a high school junior and one of the best players on the Isidore Newman **varsity** football team. He still played other positions at times. But his focus on improving at wide receiver really paid off. He snagged 45 passes for 743 yards that year. He also caught

10 touchdown passes. Odell's great season drew the attention of college **scouts** from all around the United States.

Odell enjoyed other sports in high school too. He played basketball all four years at Isidore Newman. Like his mother, he also excelled at track and field. In 2010, he took part in the Newman Invitational Track and Field Meet at his school. He won first place in the 200-meter dash and took second place in the **long jump**.

Athletic director Billy Fitzgerald oversaw all sports activity at Isidore Newman during Odell's time at the school.

Odell's senior year football season was his best yet and one of the greatest ever for an Isidore Newman player. He caught 50 passes in 2010, and 19 of them were touchdowns! His catches accounted for 1,010 yards. In Isidore Newman history, only Cooper Manning had ever caught passes for that many yards in a season.

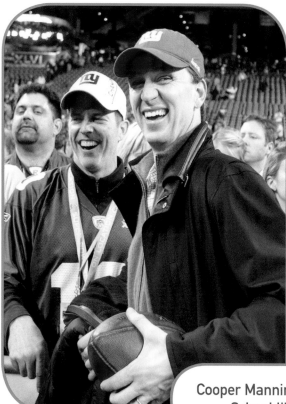

After the incredible year, Odell needed to make a decision about college.

Cooper Manning (*right*) attended Isidore Newman School like his brothers Peyton and Eli.

Many schools wanted to add the young receiver to their team. He received interest from colleges with top football teams such as the University of Nebraska and the University of Mississippi. LSU also made him an offer. It was an easy decision for Odell. He chose to join the team his dad had played for: the LSU Tigers.

The LSU campus is in Baton Rouge, Louisiana.

Odell runs with the ball during a 2011 LSU game.

In 2011 and 2012, Odell had good seasons with LSU. Then, in 2013, he became a college football star. Odell's motto that year was "don't blink." "That's because if you're at home watching on TV and step away for a second, you might miss an exciting play," he said.

During the third quarter of LSU's first home game of the 2013 season, Odell had already caught three

LSU has won the college football national championship four times: 1908, 1958, 2003, and 2007.

touchdown passes. The other team lined up for a long field goal. It was short, and Odell caught the ball in the end zone. He ran to his right, then cut to his left. He raced down the side of the field for another touchdown!

Odell reaches for a catch as an LSU wide receiver.

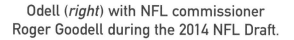

Odell (*right*) with NFL commissioner
Roger Goodell during the 2014 NFL Draft.

THE CATCH

The 2013 season was full of highlights for
Odell. When it was over, he decided to leave
LSU and enter the 2014 NFL **Draft**. The New
York Giants chose him as the 12th pick in the

first round. His longtime dream of joining the NFL had come true! The Giants were thrilled to get a player like Odell. "We can count on him to help us score some points," said New York coach Tom Coughlin.

Odell helped score some points right away. He scored a touchdown in his first NFL game. A few weeks later, he gained 156 yards against the Indianapolis Colts.

When the Giants played the Dallas Cowboys on November 23, 2014, Odell was in the middle of a fantastic **rookie** season. With no score in the game, he caught a short touchdown pass. After a Dallas field goal, New York had the ball again.

The Giants and the Cowboys have played against each other 108 times. The Cowboys won 62 of those games.

They moved it to the Cowboys' 43-yard line.

On the first play of the second quarter, New York quarterback Eli Manning ran to the right. Eli launched a pass deep down the side of the field. Odell was there, but a Cowboys player was holding his left arm. As the ball sailed over Odell's head, he reached up

Odell (*right*) makes an amazing catch for a touchdown against the Cowboys in 2014.

with one hand and snatched it out of the air. Somehow, the ball stuck to his hand. Odell fell into the end zone, and the referee raised his arms to signal a touchdown!

Odell's NFL career really took off after his 2014 touchdown catch against the Cowboys.

FAME

Fans and players alike were stunned by Odell's catch against the Cowboys. "That may be the greatest catch I've ever seen," said TV announcer and former wide receiver Cris Collinsworth. The Giants lost the game, 31–28. But Odell's catch will live on in NFL history.

In December 2014, the jersey he wore during the game was placed in the Pro Football Hall of Fame. Text near the jersey calls the play "arguably one of the best catches of all time."

Odell became incredibly popular after the catch. He appeared on TV sports shows and talk shows. He posed for photos for *ESPN The Magazine*. Odell wasn't used to so much attention, but he took it in stride. "I wouldn't trade it for the world," he said.

In July 2015, Odell won an ESPY award for "Best Play" for his stunning catch against the Cowboys.

The Giants didn't make the playoffs in 2014, but it was still a successful season for Odell. In addition to his amazing catch, he was voted Offensive Rookie of the Year. He was also voted to play in the **Pro Bowl**.

Odell runs the ball for his team during the 2015 Pro Bowl game.

In 2015, the Giants' record was no better than it had been the year before. But they still had a chance at the playoffs if they could beat the Washington Redskins in November. Washington shut down New York for most of the game. After three quarters, Washington had the lead, 20–0.

The Giants got a touchdown to make the score 20–7. When they had the ball again, they pushed down the field. With 21 yards to go for a touchdown, Eli Manning saw Odell on the left side. Manning hurled the ball, but the throw was too long. Or was it? Odell stretched with his left hand. He tapped the football to himself as his feet left the field. He wrapped both hands around the ball before crashing into the ground.

Odell makes a one-handed touchdown catch against the Redskins.

It was another fantastic touchdown! But Odell's score wasn't enough. The Giants lost the game, 20–14.

New York fans have a lot to look forward to with Odell on the field. They want to see more stunning plays like his Hall of Fame catch against the Cowboys. "I hope it's not the greatest catch of all time," Odell said. "I hope I can make more."

Odell made many big touchdown catches in his first year with the Giants.

Selected Career Highlights

2015   Voted to the Pro Bowl for the second time
Caught 96 passes for 1,450 yards and 13
touchdowns with the Giants

2014   Voted NFL Offensive Rookie of the Year
Voted to the Pro Bowl for the first time
Caught 91 passes for 1,305 yards and 12
touchdowns with the Giants
Chosen as the 12th overall pick in the NFL draft by the Giants

2013   Caught 59 passes for 1,152 yards and 8 touchdowns with LSU
Ran back a missed field goal 100 yards for a touchdown

2012   Caught 43 passes for 713 yards and 2 touchdowns with LSU
Ran back two punts for touchdowns

2011   Caught 41 passes for 475 yards and 2 touchdowns with LSU
Decided to attend LSU

2010   Caught 50 passes for 1,010 yards and 19 touchdowns with
Isidore Newman
Ran back two punts for touchdowns
Won the 200-meter dash and placed second in the long jump at the
Newman Invitational Track and Field Meet

2009   Caught 45 passes for 743 yards and 10 touchdowns with
Isidore Newman

Glossary

defense: the team that is trying to stop the other team from scoring during a football game

division: a group of teams that play against one another

draft: a yearly event in which teams take turns choosing new players from a group

end zone: the area beyond the goal line at each end of a football field. A team scores a touchdown when they reach the other team's end zone with the ball.

field goals: kicks that go between the poles at the end of a football field. A field goal is worth three points.

long jump: a track-and-field event in which athletes jump as far as they can

offense: the team that is trying to score during a football game

playoffs: a series of games played to decide a league's championship team

Pro Bowl: a game played at the end of each NFL season. The best players in the league are voted to play in the Pro Bowl.

professional: paid to play a sport

punts: kicks that result in the other team taking possession of the ball

quarterback: a football player whose main job is to throw passes

rookie: a first-year player

running back: a football player whose main job is to run with the ball

scouts: football experts who watch players to judge their abilities

varsity: the top sports team at a school

wide receiver: a football player whose main job is to catch passes

Further Reading & Websites

Braun, Eric. *Super Football Infographics*. Minneapolis: Lerner Publications, 2015.

Kennedy, Mike, and Mark Stewart. *Touchdown: The Power and Precision of Football's Perfect Play*. Minneapolis: Millbrook Press, 2010.

Savage, Jeff. *Peyton Manning*. Minneapolis: Lerner Publications, 2013.

Odell Beckham Jr. Official Website
http://www.odellbeckhamjr13.com
Learn about the latest news in Odell's life at his official website.

Official Site of the National Football League
http://www.nfl.com
The NFL's official website provides fans with recent news stories, statistics, biographies of players and coaches, and information about games.

The Official Website of the New York Giants
http://www.giants.com
The official website of the Giants includes team schedules, news, profiles of past and present players and coaches, and much more.

Sports Illustrated Kids
http://www.sikids.com
The *Sports Illustrated Kids* website covers all sports, including football.

LERNER

SOURCE

Expand learning beyond the printed book. Download free, complementary educational resources for this book from our website, www.lernerresource.com.

Index

Photo Acknowledgments

The images in this book are used with the permission of: © Chris Trotman/Getty Images, pp. 4, 5; © Mike Ehrmann/Getty Images, pp. 6, 7; © iStockphoto.com/Sam Camp, p. 9; © Louisiana State/Collegiate Images/Getty Images, pp. 11, 17; AP Photo/Jonathan Bachman/NFL, p. 12; Wade Payne/Cal Sport Media/Newscom, p. 14; AP Photo/Pat Semansky, p. 15; Chad Ryan/Cal Sport Media/Newscom, p. 16; AP Photo/Jonathan Bachman/Cal Sport Media, p. 18; AP Photo/Tony Gutierrez, p. 19; AP Photo/Tomasso DeRosa, p. 20; AP Photo/Kathy Willens, p. 22; AP Photo/Julio Cortez, p. 24; AP Photo/Perry Knotts, p. 26; AP Photo/Evan Pinkus, pp. 27, 29; AP Photo/Bill Kostroun, p. 28.

Front cover: © Rob Leiter/Getty Images.

Main body text set in Caecilia LT Std 55 Roman 16/28.
Typeface provided by Adobe Systems.